The Elements of English

THE ELEMENTS OF ENGLISH

A Glossary of Basic Terms for Literature, Composition, and Grammar

Stan Malless
Jeff McQuain

Madison Books
Lanham • New York • London

Madison Books

4720 Boston Way
Lanham, MD 20706

3 Henrietta Street
London WC2E 8LU England

This is a completely revised and expanded version
of a University Press of America book
entitled *A HANDLIST TO ENGLISH; BASIC TERMS FOR
LITERATURE, COMPOSITION, AND GRAMMAR,* published in 1986.

Library of Congress Cataloging-in-Publication Data

Malless, Stan, 1947–
The elements of English : a glossary of basic terms for
literature, composition, and grammar / Stan Malless, Jeff McQuain.
p. cm.
Rev. and expanded ed. of: A handlist to English. 1986.
Bibliography: p.
Includes index.
1. English philology—Terminology. 2. Literature—Terminology.
3. English language—Rhetoric—Terminology. 4. Rhetoric—
Terminology. 5. English language—Grammar—Terminology.
I. McQuain, Jeff, 1955   . II. Malless, Stan, 1947   Handlist of
English. III. Title.
[PE31.M35   1988]
801.4—dc 19   88-5149 CIP
ISBN 0–8191–6803–3 (pbk. : alk. paper)

All Madison Books are produced on acid-free
paper which exceeds the minimum standards set by the National
Historical Publications and Records Commission.

To Norine Wolf and Genetta McQuain

Contents

Acknowledgments

We thank the following people for their selfless giving of time, advice, and encouragement: Betsy Butler, English teacher, Richard Montgomery High School, Rockville, Md.; Thomas F. Cannon, Jr., Assistant Professor of Literature, The American University, Washington, D.C.; Marguerite Coley, English and drama teacher, Winston Churchill High School, Potomac, Md.; Lynda Foro, editorial director, *Words From Home*, Phoenix, Ariz.; Hans Gaussman, English teacher and department chairperson, Seneca Valley High School, Germantown, Md.; Rikki Hall, former student, Seneca Valley High School; Linda Henke, Curriculum Director, West Des Moines Community School District, West Des Moines, Ia.; Todd Lieber, fiction writer and Professor of English, Simpson College, Indianola, Ia.; George C. Malless, Specialist in Guidance, Maryland State Department of Education, Baltimore, Md.; Phyllis Parks Malless, poet, editor, devoted wife, and English teacher, Stilwell Junior High School, West Des Moines, Ia.; Rosamond Kent Sprague, Professor of Philosophy, University of South Carolina, Columbia, S.C.; Mary Tonkinson, *The Shakespeare Quarterly*, The Folger Library, Washington, D.C. We are indebted to these colleagues and friends for the strengths of this book; for its weaknesses we are solely responsible.

Preface to the Second Edition
(The Elements of English: A Glossary of Basic Terms for Literature, Composition, and Grammar)

Since the summer of 1986, when this book first appeared as *A Handlist to English: Basic Terms for Literature, Composition, and Grammar*, two books on American education have become bestsellers: *Cultural Literacy* by E. D. Hirsch, Jr., and *The Closing of the American Mind* by Allan Bloom. They are the latest in what has become, during the 1980's, a serial indictment of American education generally and American education curricula specifically. Although both books have helped us to better understand our suspicions that American education may be, in some ways, out of focus, Professor Hirsch's thesis proved particularly to be attuned to our own idea for *A Handlist*. He maintains that learning is based upon "cultural literacy" or a "shared national vocabulary." Our attempt to develop such a core vocabulary, however, was aimed at the English classroom, whether traditional or whole language, and its interrelated areas of literature, composition, grammar, and discussion.

We interviewed students and teachers from elementary and secondary schools and from colleges and universities; researched glossaries, handbooks, textbooks, and curriculum guides; and reviewed our own combined teaching experience in public schools (remedial and average-level literature, composition, and grammar courses, as well as sections of gifted and talented, honors, and advanced-placement students) and in colleges and universities (composition and literature courses). Our objective was to compile a list of basic terms for literature, composition, and grammar—common, non-specialized terms that most students from 7th grade to 12th grade, regardless of ability grouping, would have been exposed to and expected to be familiar with by graduation from high school.

This revised edition has enlarged upon that objective in three specific ways. First, we reconsidered each definition and revised as necessary to insure that every definition is the one most commonly taught. Second, to supplement our original core vocabulary, we included—as main entries, subentries, or examples—appropriate terms, names, and expressions that Professor Hirsch has included in his "What Literate Americans Know, A Preliminary List." (Most of the language-arts terms on that list were included in our original *Handlist*.) Third, to make this book more useful in the classroom, we have included sections on basic rules for capitalization and punctuation. We have also added a list of those works we consulted.

Stan Malless
Jeff McQuain
October 1987

Preface to the First Edition
(A Handlist to English: Basic Terms for Literature, Composition, and Grammar)

As teachers of high school and college English, we have been made uncomfortably aware each year of the need for *A Handlist to English: Basic Terms for Literature, Composition, and Grammar*. Unfortunately, many current glossaries cover only one area of the language arts: literature *or* composition *or* grammar; these glossaries tend to be lengthy and complicated, often leaving students confused. Therefore, our purpose was to compose a handlist of brief yet precise definitions for the *basic* terms in all three areas of the high school and introductory college English curriculum.

That purpose guided the working strategy for our *Handlist*. We researched the current English language-arts textbooks, curriculum guides, handbooks (both in and out of print), and dictionaries. Also, we consulted a representative cross-section of both students and teachers (Grades 8–12 and introductory college level) to select only those terms that are required of the *majority* of high school students as well as college freshmen. We then wrote an original definition for each term. In every definition, we tried to strike a balance between keeping the entry concise and explaining the term clearly. Five years ago, we began this *Handlist*, well knowing that definitions are never unanimously accepted but that definitions are always unanimously needed.

As convenient for students as a classroom handout, our *Handlist* is comparatively brief. Thus, it will be very helpful as a means of quick review for both the desperate student before test time and the perplexed parent at homework time. To expedite that "quick review" even further, we have added an index that lists alphabetically not only the basic terms but also some of the not-so-basic terms that we found necessary to include within the main entries.

Finally, teachers of English will find our *Handlist* helpful because of its comprehensiveness and brevity. In fact, as teachers across the curriculum look for ways to improve language-arts skills, the need for texts both useful and usable in and out of the classroom increases. We believe that *A Handlist to English* satisfies this need.

Stan Malless
Jeff McQuain
June 1985

I.
Literature—
the *art* of written communication

allegory—a story developed through characters, places, and events that often represent concepts such as good and evil. In a common type of *allegory*, a "good" character or place has a name with "good" connotations (Virtue or Humility), and a bad character or place has a name with "bad" connotations (Vice or Vanity); the personality of each character or the quality of each place is defined by the meaning of the name of that character or place. For example, in the 19th-century American short story "Young Goodman Brown" by Nathaniel Hawthorne, the main character, Goodman Brown, is a good man, and his wife, Faith, is faithful, but when Goodman Brown enters a dark and gloomy forest, his goodness is tested. Also, the events of an allegory are metaphorical. The slaying of a dragon, for instance, can represent the triumph of good over evil.

TIP: An allegory is a type of metaphor that often teaches a moral lesson.

alliteration—the repetition of the same first sound, either consonant or vowel, in two or more words. These words must be either side-by-side or very close together. *Allit-*

eration is used, for example, in the title of a famous 17th-century English allegory by John Bunyan, *The Pilgrim's Progress*. Following are other examples of alliteration:
1. "Sounds of Silence" (two words very close together)
2. The source was cited (two words beginning with the same sound but different letters)
3. "East of Eden" (two words beginning with the same vowel sound).

allusion—a reference to either someone or something (historical or fictional) in a work of literature when that someone or something does not appear in that work.
EXAMPLE: A work of literature about a 20th-century heroine might include this sentence: "She has the wisdom of Athena." The *allusion* is to the Greek mythological goddess Athena, who is referred to but is not a character in the work itself.

ambiguity—more than one meaning. In a work of literature, a word or a gesture can have more than one meaning at the same time. One example of *ambiguity* is the word "right" because it can mean both "correct" and "opposite to left" at the same time, as in the sentence "Be sure to take the right turn."
NOTE: A famous book on ambiguity in literature is *The Seven Types of Ambiguity* by the 20th-century English critic William Empson.

anachronism—any person or thing described as existing in a period of history other than its own. For example, the title of a 19th-century novel by the American writer Mark Twain, *A Connecticut Yankee in King Arthur's Court*, includes an *anachronism*.

analogy—any type of expression that describes one pair of unlike things as if it were another pair of unlike things, without specifically stating how those pairs are similar.

EXAMPLE of *analogy*: Laughing is to comedy as crying is to tragedy.
KEEP IN MIND: Analogy is a figure of speech.

antagonist—the character in a story who opposes the main character of that story. For example, in the Anglo-Saxon narrative poem *Beowulf*, the monster Grendel is an *antagonist* because Grendel opposes the main character of the story, Beowulf.
TIP: Sometimes the antagonist in a story is referred to as the *villain* of that story.

anthology—a collection (in one book) of various works of literature.
HINT: Often a literature textbook is an *anthology*.

apostrophe—words spoken to someone or something that the speaker knows is physically not present. One example of an *apostrophe* is found in the famous narrative poem *The Divine Comedy* by the 14th-century Italian poet Dante Alighieri:
"O clear conscience and upright! How
doth a little failing wound thee sore."
(Purgatory, III, 8, translated by Henry F. Cary)
TIP: Perhaps the oldest form of apostrophe is a prayer.

aside—in drama, a character's thoughts spoken out loud by that character when other characters are also on stage. The *aside* is heard by the audience, but not by all of the characters on stage.

assonance—the repetition in two or more words of the same vowel sound, which is followed by a different consonant sound in each word. *Assonance* requires that these words be either side-by-side or very close together.
EXAMPLE: In "The rain-maker made rain," note that "rain," "maker," and "made" all have the same

vowel sound. In each word, however, that vowel sound is followed by a different consonant sound.

autobiography—the history of a person's life written by that person. For example, in Benjamin Franklin's *Autobiography*, Franklin himself wrote the history of his life.

> KEEP IN MIND: The word "autobiography" comes from the following roots:
> > "auto" (self) + "bio" (life) + "graph" (to write) = "To write (about) the life of one's self."

ballad—a popular, medium-length rhyming poem that tells a story. The traditional *ballad* form has an *abcb* rhyme scheme and four-line stanzas of alternating four-beat/three-beat iambic lines, but there are many variations of this form.

> EXAMPLE of a ballad stanza:
> > "They hadna sail'd a league, a league,
> > > A league but barely three,
> > When the lift grew dark, and the wind blew loud,
> > > And gurly grew the sea."
> > > > ("Sir Patrick Spens," XI)
> NOTE: The early stories of Robin Hood were sung as *folk ballads* and had anonymous authors. (There are many Robin Hood ballads.) On the other hand, the author of a *literary ballad*, which is an imitation of the folk ballad, is a named poet. The 19th-century English poet Samuel Taylor Coleridge's "The Rime of the Ancient Mariner," for example, is a well-known literary ballad that is similar to the folk ballad quoted above, "Sir Patrick Spens."

biography—the history of a person's life written by someone other than that person. For example, the 20th-century American poet Carl Sandburg wrote a lengthy *biography* of Abraham Lincoln.

> KEEP IN MIND: The word "biography" comes from the following roots:

"bio" (life) + "graph" (to write) =
"To write (about) someone's life."

blank verse—lines of poetry that do not end in rhyme but do
have approximately the same number of syllables in each
line (that is, they have the same meter, usually iambic
pentameter). The most famous examples of *blank verse*
may be found in Shakespeare's plays:

"To be, or not to be, that is the question:
Whether 'tis nobler in the mind to suffer
The slings and arrows of outrageous fortune,
Or to take arms against a sea of troubles,
And by opposing, end them. . . ."

(*Hamlet*, III, i, 55–59)

catastrophe—the fatal action that occurs near the end of a
tragedy and involves the main characters. Usually the
catastrophe is either the death or the downfall of the hero/
heroine or the villain or both of those characters. In
Shakespeare's *Romeo and Juliet*, for example, the catastrophe is the death of both Romeo and Juliet. In another
example, *Death of a Salesman*, by the 20th-century American playwright Arthur Miller, the catastrophe is the
death of Willy Loman in the final act of the play.
NOTE: What is referred to in tragedy as catastrophe can
be referred to in comedy as denouement.

catharsis—a term used by the ancient Greek philosopher
Aristotle to describe the emotional release of pity and
fear that a tragedy makes us feel. When a good character
suffers in a tragedy, we fear for as well as pity that
character's life, as we do, for example, the life of Oedipus
in Sophocles's tragedy *Oedipus Rex*.
TIP: The literal meaning of *catharsis* is "cleansing" or
"purification."

classicism—a term that refers to the principles of ancient

Greek and Roman art (literature, sculpture, and architecture). Classical Greek authors who influenced English literature include the epic poet Homer (*Iliad* and *Odyssey*), the historian Herodotus (*Histories*), the philosophers Plato (*Republic*) and Aristotle (*Poetics*), and the dramatist Sophocles (*Oedipus Rex*). Classical Roman authors include the orator Cicero (*De Oratore*), the poet-critic Horace (*Ars Poetica*), and the epic poet Virgil (*Aeneid*).
NOTE: *Classicism* was at its height of imitation in English literature during the 18th century, a period referred to as the Neoclassical (or "New" classical) Age.

climax—in traditional drama, the crucial event that occurs at approximately the midpoint in the plot of a play. The *climax* is usually the turning point (or "point of no return") for the main character; from this point on, that character's life takes a turn either for the best (a comedy) or for the worst (a tragedy). In Shakespeare's tragedy *Julius Caesar*, for example, the climax occurs for Brutus when Mark Antony gives his "Friends, Romans, countrymen" speech at Caesar's funeral (III, ii).

comedy—a type of drama in which the main characters are united in a happy ending. In *comedy*, the main characters are traditionally good people who fall prey to an error in judgment; however, because that error is recognized before it leads to their downfall, those characters are, in the end, united, often in marriage. Shakespeare wrote a number of comedies, and among those still read and performed today are *As You Like It*, *Much Ado About Nothing*, *The Comedy of Errors*, and *Twelfth Night*.

conflict—in narrative or drama, the opposition between protagonist (hero/heroine) and antagonist (villain). The three basic types of *conflict* are person-versus-person (William Golding's novel *Lord of the Flies*); person-versus-nature (Ernest Hemingway's novel *The Old Man and the*

Sea); and self-versus-self (Stephen Crane's *The Red Badge of Courage*).

consonance—the repetition in two or more words of the same consonant sound. Usually *consonance* occurs in the middle of words, unlike alliteration, which repeats the same consonant sound at the beginning of words. Consonance requires that these words be either side-by-side or very close together.
EXAMPLES:
1. "What so proudly we hailed at the twilight's last gleaming."
2. "Stands tiptoe on the misty mountaintops."

couplet—two consecutive lines of poetry that end in rhyme and also have approximately the same number of syllables in each line (that is, they have the same meter, usually iambic pentameter). Alexander Pope, the 18th-century English poet-critic, is generally considered the master of the *couplet* form. The following couplet is from his "Essay on Criticism":
"True wit is Nature to advantage dress'd,
What oft was thought, but ne'er so well express'd."
NOTICE: Pope's couplet is also an epigram.
TIP: Each of Shakespeare's sonnets ends in a couplet.

denouement—in a tragedy, the action that follows the climax and "unties" the plot of the play. The *denouement* in Shakespeare's *Julius Caesar*, for example, is the action following Antony's speech at Caesar's funeral; this action determines not only how Brutus will die but also who will finally rule Rome.
TIP: The denouement of a tragedy is also the falling action of that tragedy.
NOTE: In a comedy, "denouement" can refer to the final scene that "unties" those "knots" of confusion (such as mistaken identities) that develop throughout the plot of a comedy.

drama—any performance using action and dialogue to imitate life. Every play is a work of *drama;* however, drama can also occur in narratives and poetry.

KEEP IN MIND: Drama is a genre of literature.

elegy—a lyric poem that mourns the dead. An *elegy* is an entire poem about the loss that one feels after someone or something has died. One famous elegy is "Elegy Written in a Country Churchyard" by the 18th-century English poet Thomas Gray.

TIP: Long works of literature that are not elegies themselves may include passages that mourn the dead; these passages are called elegiac. Famous elegiac passages, for example, can be found in Homer's *Iliad* and *Odyssey*.

epic—a long and involved work of narrative poetry that tells the most heroic of stories in its nation's cultural history. Famous *epics* include the ancient Greek *Iliad* and *Odyssey* by Homer, the classical Roman *Aeneid* by Virgil, and the 17th-century English *Paradise Lost* by John Milton.

BEWARE: Sometimes an epic is translated from poetry into prose and might be mistaken for a novel.

epigram—a very brief, witty poem or saying. The *epigram* has been compared to a scorpion, because, like the scorpion, the epigram has a "sting" (wit) in its "tail" (conclusion).

EXAMPLE:

"What is an epigram? a dwarfish whole.
Its body brevity, and wit its soul."

(Samuel Taylor Coleridge)

epithet—a descriptive expression that labels a person or thing throughout a work of literature. *Epithets* are commonly found in epics. For example, the ancient Greek *Odyssey* by Homer includes the following epithets: "long-suffering Odysseus," "rosy-fingered Dawn," "bright-eyed Athena," and "much-nourishing earth."

euphemism—any polite word or expression that is substituted for another word or expression that someone might

find vulgar, offensive, or embarrassing. Common examples of *euphemism* are "restroom" for "toilet" and "passed away" for "died."
KEEP IN MIND: Euphemism is a figure of speech.

falling action—in traditional drama, all of the action that follows the climax of a play. *Falling action* begins when the main character's life takes a turn either for the best (a comedy) or for the worst (a tragedy).
NOTE: The falling action in a tragedy can be referred to as the tragedy's denouement.

fiction—a make-believe story. *Fiction* can be written in either prose or poetry.

figure of speech—any type of expression that is metaphorical (not literal). *Figures of speech* (or *figurative language*) include the following types: analogy, euphemism, hyperbole, irony, metaphor, metonymy, oxymoron, paradox, personification, simile, and synecdoche.

folklore—tales, legends, proverbs, superstitions, rituals, ballads, and myths. These are among the many beliefs and customs that are, collectively, referred to as *folklore*. For the most part, folklore is anonymous and is orally transmitted from generation to generation.

foreshadowing—a hint of things to come in the plot of a story. *Foreshadowing* occurs whenever a future event in a story is hinted at or suggested by someone or something in that story. For example, in the short story "To Build a Fire" by the early 20th-century novelist-adventurer Jack London, upcoming disaster is foreshadowed by the depressed behavior of the protagonist's dog.

free verse—lines of poetry that neither end in rhyme nor have a consistent, recognizable meter but are, nonetheless, rhythmical. A famous poem written in *free verse* is

"Song of Myself" by the 19th-century American poet
Walt Whitman. It begins,
"I celebrate myself, and sing myself,
And what I assume you shall assume,
For every atom belonging to me as good
           belongs to you. . . ." (1, 1–3)

genre—a category into which a work of literature is grouped.
The three broadest examples of *genre* are poetry, narrative, and drama, but genre is not always limited to these.
Other genres are lyric, epic, novel, tragedy, comedy,
essay, etc.

hamartia—a term used by the ancient Greek philosopher
Aristotle to describe the misjudgment of a tragic hero
that ultimately causes his suffering and death. For example, *hamartia* is found in Shakespeare's *Macbeth* when
Macbeth misjudges the witches' prophecies and in so
doing brings about his tragic suffering and death.
TIP: Hamartia is often referred to as *tragic flaw* or "error
in judgment" and is usually associated with a fatal
weakness in character.

hero/heroine—traditionally the main character in a work of
literature who, against all odds, struggles to overcome
his or her antagonist or antagonists (another person,
nature, self). Two specific types of *heroes and heroines* are
the epic and the tragic. The *epic hero/heroine* is an almost
superhuman figure who overcomes antagonists throughout the epic (Odysseus in Homer's *Odyssey* and perhaps
Scarlett O'Hara in Margaret Mitchell's *Gone with the
Wind*). In contrast, the *tragic hero/heroine*, because of a
mistake in judgment or weakness in character, becomes
a victim of his or her own acts. When the tragic hero/
heroine recognizes this mistake, it is too late to correct it,
but he or she does struggle to overcome the final defeat
(Macbeth in Shakespeare's *Macbeth*).

hubris—an ancient Greek word for the fatal weakness of uncontrollable pride. For example, the *hubris* of Achilles in Homer's *Iliad* causes his downfall and death.
NOTE: Hubris is often associated with hamartia.

hyperbole—an over-exaggerated description of something.
EXAMPLE: In the statement "I'd give the world to see that movie," the speaker cannot really give the world to see a movie but uses *hyperbole* to exaggerate how strongly he or she feels about seeing it.
KEEP IN MIND: Hyperbole is a figure of speech.

iambic pentameter—any line of poetry that contains approximately ten syllables arranged in a specific pattern. The pattern for *iambic pentameter* is an unaccented syllable (˘) followed by an accented syllable (´); this pattern must occur five times in the same line. The following line from the 19th-century English poet Alfred Lord Tennyson's poem "Ulysses" is in iambic pentameter:
"Tŏ stríve, tŏ séek, tŏ fínd, ănd nót tŏ yíeld."
NOTE: Iambic pentameter is the most commonly written line of poetry in English.

imagery—the descriptive use of detail to appeal to one or more of the reader's senses or to create a picture in the reader's mind. *Imagery* helps the reader to "see" and "feel" a character or a setting in a work of literature.
EXAMPLE of imagery from "The Rime of the Ancient Mariner" by the 19th-century poet-critic Samuel Taylor Coleridge:
"Beyond the shadow of the ship,
I watched the water-snakes:
They moved in tracks of shining white,
And when they reared, the elfish light
Fell off in hoary flakes.

Within the shadow of the ship

> I watched their rich attire:
> Blue, glossy green, and velvet black
> They coiled and swam; and every track
> Was a flash of golden fire." (272–281)

in medias res—a Latin phrase that means "into the middle of things." *In medias res* describes the way that an epic's plot usually begins: the story begins with action that occurs *after* the beginning of the plot.

> TIP: A story that begins in medias res is using a narrative technique similar to the *flashback* because, like the flashback, in medias res takes the reader backward in the time of the story.

irony—the occurrence of the opposite of what is intended or expected. There are three main types of *irony*:

1. *Verbal irony* occurs when what a speaker says is deliberately the opposite of what is true. For example, in Shakespeare's *Julius Caesar*, Mark Antony uses verbal irony when he describes Caesar's assassins as "honorable men"; he believes the opposite is true—that they are, in fact, dishonorable men.

2. *Dramatic irony* occurs when the audience or reader is aware that the opposite of what a character expects will either happen or be true. For example, in Shakespeare's *Romeo and Juliet*, dramatic irony occurs in the final act when Romeo thinks Juliet is dead, but the audience knows the opposite is true—that Juliet, in fact, is still alive.

3. *Situational irony* occurs when a person or an audience expects one thing to happen or be true but is unaware that the opposite will happen or be true instead. The surprise endings of some of O. Henry's short stories ("The Gift of the Magi") are examples of situational irony.

> KEEP IN MIND: Irony (especially verbal irony) is a figure of speech.

lyric—typically a short song-like poem that is not a narrative. The *lyric* has both a personal quality and a musical quality and is often about a single emotion; for example, Shakespeare's sonnets are musical and describe personal feelings about love. The most common forms of the lyric are elegy, ode, *song*, and sonnet.

NOTICE: The lyrics to a popular song can be read as a short poem.

metaphor—any type of expression that describes a person or a thing as if it were a different person or thing. For example, Shakespeare's well-known line "All the world's a stage" is a *metaphor* because a thing ("the world") is described as if it were a different thing ("a stage").

WARNING: An expression using "like" or "as" to relate two unlike things ("The world is like a stage") is called a simile.

KEEP IN MIND: Metaphor is a figure of speech.

meter (metrical foot)—in poetry, one measure of a rhythm. This measure, or *meter*, requires that a specific order of accented (˘) and unaccented (´) syllables be repeated throughout the lines of a poem. There are four main types of meter:

   1. *iambic* (˘´): "Shĕ wálks ĭn béautў likĕ thĕ níght."
   2. *trochaic* (´˘): "Dóublĕ, dóublĕ, tóil ănd tróublĕ."
   3. *anapestic* (˘˘´): "Ĭn thĕ lánd ŏf thĕ frée ănd thĕ hóme ŏf thĕ bráve."
   4. *dactylic* (´˘˘): "Cómĕdў, trágĕdў, hístŏrў, pástŏrăl."

NOTE: The number of *metrical feet* in a single line of poetry is indicated by a Greek prefix:

   1. *mono-* (one)—monometer
   2. *di-* (two)—dimeter
   3. *tri-* (three)—trimeter
   4. *tetra-* (four)—tetrameter
   5. *penta-* (five)—pentameter
   6. *hexa-* (six)—hexameter.

KEEP IN MIND: When you read a line of poetry to

determine its meter, you are *scanning* that line of poetry (*scansion*). For example, the four quotations above are in tetrameter; therefore, they are described as "iambic tetrameter," "trochaic tetrameter," "anapestic tetrameter," and "dactylic tetrameter."

metonymy—any type of expression that describes a person or a thing as if it were something very closely associated with that person or thing.
EXAMPLES of *metonymy*:
1. We refer to top military officers as "the brass" because the brass on their uniforms is closely associated with the officers themselves.
2. We refer to a mystery story as "cloak-and-dagger" because both cloaks and daggers are very closely associated with that type of story.
KEEP IN MIND: Metonymy is a figure of speech.

Middle English—the English language that was written and spoken between approximately A.D. 1100 and A.D. 1500.
NOTE: The most famous work in *Middle English* is Geoffrey Chaucer's narrative poem *The Canterbury Tales*, which begins,
    "Whan that Aprill with his shoures soote. . . ."
    ("When that April with its showers sweet. . . .")
TIP: Middle English led into *Modern English*, the current period of our language.

myth—a story (in poetry or prose) in which the nature of all things, including human nature, is influenced by gods and goddesses. Because the classical *myths* were early forms of art, religion, history, science, and psychology, they have had a strong influence on the development of literature in the Western world.

narrative—any story that someone tells. In literature, a *narrative* can be a novel, a short story, a ballad, or an epic. Most narratives include *characterization* (the people in the story), *setting* (the time and place of the story), and *plot* (the author's plan for what happens in the story). *Dialogue*, the conversation between two or more characters, is common but is not required in a narrative.

TIP: A narrative is told by a narrator.

CAUTION: A play is a story but is not a narrative because the play is performed, not simply told by a narrator.

KEEP IN MIND: Narrative is a genre of literature.

REMEMBER: Narrative writing *(narration)* is one of the four types of discourse: argumentation, description, exposition, and narration.

narrator—in a narrative, the person who tells the story. A *narrator* tells the story from a specific *point of view;* the most common are the following:

1. *first-person* ("I")—a person in the story tells the story from only his or her viewpoint, as in the novel *A Separate Peace* by John Knowles

2. *third-person limited* ("he"/"she"/"it")—the narrator tells the story from the point of view of one character in the story who is not the narrator, as in George Orwell's novel *1984*

3. *third-person omniscient* ("he"/"she"/"it")—the narrator is "all-knowing" and interprets the thoughts and feelings of one or more characters in the story, as in Margaret Mitchell's novel *Gone with the Wind.*

BEWARE: Both first-person and third-person pronouns are used in dialogue. Narrative portions of a work, not dialogue, determine point of view.

NOTE: One other point of view is *third-person objective,* which is rarely used in fiction. From this point of view, the narrator is like a newspaper reporter who describes but does not interpret.

neoclassicism—a term that refers in particular to the art of English literature written between the mid-1600's and the mid–1700's. Neoclassical works are balanced, logical, and in some ways "scientific." Famous English writers of the Neoclassical Age include John Dryden, Alexander Pope, Jonathan Swift, and Samuel Johnson; famous American writers of this period include Benjamin Franklin, Thomas Jefferson, and James Madison.

> NOTICE: *Neoclassicism* is a "new" ("neo" = "new") classicism—that is, a new appreciation of the principles of ancient Greek and Roman art.

novel—a long prose-fiction narrative. The *novel* is longer than the short story because, generally, the novel is an attempt to create more than one effect within a narrative unity. Some famous English novels are the 18th-century *Tom Jones* by Henry Fielding, the 19th-century *Pride and Prejudice* by Jane Austen and *Great Expectations* by Charles Dickens, and the early 20th-century *Heart of Darkness* by Joseph Conrad. Famous American novels include the 19th-century *The Scarlet Letter* by Nathaniel Hawthorne, *Moby Dick* by Herman Melville, and *Huckleberry Finn* by Mark Twain (Samuel Clemens); among the 20th-century American novels are *The Great Gatsby* by F. Scott Fitzgerald, *The Sun Also Rises* by Ernest Hemingway, *The Catcher in the Rye* by J. D. Salinger, and *The Color Purple* by Alice Walker.

octave (octet)—eight consecutive lines of poetry that together develop the same idea. An *octave*, which can vary in line length and rhyme scheme, can be a part of a longer poem or can stand as a poem by itself.

> HINT: Octaves, also called *octets*, are most often found as the first eight lines of the Petrarchan (or Italian) sonnet and have the following rhyme scheme: *ab-baabba*.

ode—a lyric poem that praises or celebrates in a dignified way a person, a thing, or an event. For the ancient Greeks the *ode* was a favorite form of poetry that was accompanied by music, singing, and dancing. Some of the best-known odes in English are from the 19th-century: John Keats's "Ode on a Grecian Urn" and "Ode to a Nightingale," and Percy Bysshe Shelley's "Ode to the West Wind."

Old English—the English language that was written and spoken between approximately A.D. 500 and A.D. 1100. *Old English* is also called *Anglo-Saxon*.
NOTE: The most famous work in Old English is the narrative poem *Beowulf*, which begins,
> "Hwaet, we Gar-Dena   in geardagum. . . ."
> ("What! we Spear-Danes   in days of yore. . . .")

onomatopoeia—a word that is invented to imitate a sound. Examples of *onomatopoeia* are words like "screech," "buzz," "clank," "boom," and "pop."

oxymoron—two words used together that have opposite meanings. Although the words in an *oxymoron* have opposite meanings, the meaning of those words together somehow still makes sense to the reader.
EXAMPLES: "killing kindness," "darkness visible," and "sweet sorrow."
KEEP IN MIND: Oxymoron is a figure of speech.

paradox—a statement that seems contradictory or illogical but does, in fact, have an understandable meaning. Some of our common expressions are examples of *paradox*.
EXAMPLES:
1. "e pluribus unum" (out of many, one)
2. "Make haste slowly"
3. "Hearing, they hear not."
KEEP IN MIND: Paradox is a figure of speech.

parody—the comic imitation of a well-known style or work. *Parody* is comical because it applies that style or adapts that work to a subject of lesser importance than the original. For example, a parody of " 'Twas the Night

Before Christmas" might begin, " 'Twas the night before finals and all through the dorm. . . ."
REMEMBER: Parody is often a form of satire.

persona—a person who is imagined to be the speaking voice of a work of literature. That person, or *persona*, is not necessarily the voice of the writer. For instance, in some of Shakespeare's sonnets, a sad lover often speaks the poem: the sad lover, not Shakespeare, is the persona of that poem.

personification—any type of expression that describes non-human things as if they were human. Many of our common expressions are examples of *personification*.
EXAMPLES:
    1. "Money talks"
    2. "Necessity is the mother of invention"
    3. "Actions speak louder than words."
THINK OF IT THIS WAY: *Person*-ification, or personification "personizes."
KEEP IN MIND: Personification is a figure of speech.

plot—the author's plan for what happens in a story. A traditional *plot* presents action as a sequence of events from the beginning of a work through its conflict to the ending of that work.
NOTE: Any story can have more than one plot: the lesser plots are called *subplots*.

poetry—ballad, blank verse, couplet, elegy, epic, free verse, lyric, ode, and sonnet. These are the most common forms of *poetry*.
NOTE: The 19th-century English poet-critic Samuel Taylor Coleridge perhaps best defined poetry as "the best words in the best order."
KEEP IN MIND: Poetry is a genre of literature.

prose—autobiography, biography, essay, magazine or news-

paper article, novel, and short story. These are the most
common forms of *prose*.
NOTE: Samuel Taylor Coleridge (see above) perhaps best
defined prose as "words in their best order."

protagonist—the main character in a story. Usually a *protagonist* is the hero or heroine of a story. For example,
Evangeline is the protagonist of the 19th-century narrative poem *Evangeline, A Tale of Acadie* by Henry Wadsworth Longfellow, and Holden Caulfield is the protagonist of the 20th-century American novel *The Catcher in the
Rye* by J. D. Salinger.

quatrain—a four-line stanza of poetry that usually develops
one idea. A *quatrain*, which can vary in line length and
rhyme scheme, can be a part of a longer poem or can
stand as a poem by itself.
HINT: Quatrains are most often found in ballads and in
Shakespearean (or English) sonnets.

Renaissance—as it applies to England and English literature,
a term that refers to the period between approximately
A.D. 1400 and A.D. 1600. Works of the *Renaissance*
throughout Europe were widely influenced by human-
ism (a strong belief in the importance of humankind),
the exploration of new worlds, and a rebirth of interest
in ancient Greek and Roman culture. ("Renaissance" is a
French word that means "rebirth.") Famous writers of
the Renaissance in England include Sir Francis Bacon, Sir
Walter Raleigh, and William Shakespeare.

rhyme—the repetition of the same middle and end sounds in
two or more words that begin with different sounds.
NOTE: The most common forms of *rhyme* are the following:
1. *Exact rhyme* occurs when two or more words
begin with different sounds but have exactly the

same middle and end sounds ("teacher"/"crea-
ture")

2. _Near rhyme_ occurs when two or more words begin
   with different sounds but have exactly the same
   final letter or a similar final sound without rhyming exactly ("mind"/"maid" or "shoulder"/"wa-
   ter")

3. _End rhyme_ occurs when the last word of one line
   rhymes exactly with the last word of another line:
   > "Double, double, toil and _trouble;_
   > Fire burn and cauldron _bubble_"

4. _Internal rhyme_ occurs when a word in the middle
   of a line rhymes exactly with another word in
   that same line:
   > "Hundreds _more_ had fallen _before._"

rhyme scheme—a way to label the rhymes that occur at the
end of different lines in a poem. A poem's _rhyme scheme_
is indicated by the use of lowercase letters, and lines that
rhyme are given the same letter. For example, the rhyme
scheme for "Humpty Dumpty" is _aabb_:

"Humpty Dumpty sat on a _wall;_	(_a_)
Humpty Dumpty had a great _fall;_	(_a_)
All the king's horses and all the king's _men_	(_b_)
Couldn't put Humpty together _again._"	(_b_)

rhythm—in poetry or prose, the repetition at regular intervals
of the same metrical pattern, image, or idea. Metrical
rhythm is based upon the repetition at regular intervals
of identical patterns of accented and unaccented syllables
(meter).

rising action—in drama, all of the action in the first half of a
play. A play's suspense builds until _rising action_ ends at
the climax, when falling action begins. Rising action
usually begins with background information, or _exposi-
tion._

romanticism—a term used to describe the art of English and American literature that was written between the late–1700's and the mid–1800's. Works of *romanticism* were widely influenced by the heroic, the supernatural, a love of nature, and an interest in medieval, gothic places that became the settings for tales of horror. Well-known English writers of the romantic period include Lord Byron, Samuel Taylor Coleridge, John Keats, Mary Shelley, Percy Bysshe Shelley, and William Wordsworth. Famous American writers of this period include Louisa May Alcott, James Fenimore Cooper, Ralph Waldo Emerson, Nathaniel Hawthorne, Washington Irving, Henry Wadsworth Longfellow, Herman Melville, Edgar Allan Poe, and Henry David Thoreau.

satire—a work of poetry or prose that uses humor to ridicule either a person or a thing in order to help change that person or thing for the better. Three of the best-known English *satires* are from the 18th century: "The Rape of the Lock" by Alexander Pope, and *Gulliver's Travels* and "A Modest Proposal" by Jonathan Swift.

sestet—six consecutive lines of poetry that together develop the same idea. A *sestet*, which can vary in line length and rhyme scheme, can be a part of a longer poem or can stand as a poem by itself.
HINT: Sestets are most often found as the final six lines of a Petrarchan (or Italian) sonnet and have the following rhyme scheme: *cdccdc* (or a variation).

short story—a brief prose-fiction narrative. The *short story* is brief because, generally, it is an attempt to create a single effect within a narrative unity. Famous American short stories include Edgar Allan Poe's 19th-century "The Telltale Heart" and "Fall of the House of Usher." Twentieth-century examples include "The Lottery" by Shirley Jackson and "Thank you, M'am" by Langston Hughes.

simile—any type of expression that relates two unlike things by using "like" or "as" to relate them. For example, "I Wandered Lonely as a Cloud," the title of a well-known 19th-century poem by William Wordsworth, is a *simile* because "as" is used to relate "I" and "Cloud."

    WARNING: Two unlike things that are related without using "like" or "as" form a metaphor.

    KEEP IN MIND: Simile is a figure of speech.

soliloquy—in drama, a character's thoughts spoken out loud by that character when he or she is alone on stage. A *soliloquy* tells the audience what that character is thinking. Perhaps the most famous soliloquy in a Shakespeare play is Hamlet's "To be, or not to be" speech (III, i, 55–87).

    CAUTION: A character's lengthy speech to other characters on stage is called a *monologue*.

    REMEMBER: A soliloquy is a solo.

sonnet—a fourteen-line lyric poem in rhymed iambic pentameter. The *sonnet* must be arranged in a specific rhyme scheme, and there are only a few possible traditional rhyme schemes from which the poet can choose.

    NOTE: Shakespeare wrote more than 150 sonnets, all of them having basically the same organization and rhyme scheme: *abab cdcd efef gg*. That particular sonnet form,which requires three quatrains and a couplet, is now called the *Shakespearean* (or *English) sonnet*. The other conventional sonnet form is the *Petrarchan* (or *Italian*) sonnet, named after the 14th-century Italian poet, Petrarch, who made it famous. The Petrarchan sonnet requires an octave and a sestet written in the following rhyme scheme: *abbaabba cdccdc* (or a variation).

stanza—consecutive lines of a poem that are set apart from the rest of the poem and form a division of that poem. A *stanza* is always a part of a longer poem and cannot stand as a poem by itself.

CAUTION: Stanzas can be of either fixed or irregular lengths. A sixteen-line poem, for example, might be divided into two eight-line stanzas; on the other hand, another sixteen-line poem might be divided into one stanza of nine lines and another stanza of seven lines.

stream-of-consciousness—a style of narration that attempts to imitate the thinking mind, with its free associations, disorganized syntax, and lack of ordinary context. Two works famous for the *stream-of-consciousness* technique are both from the 20th century: the American novel *The Sound and the Fury* by William Faulkner and the Irish novel *Ulysses* by James Joyce.

symbol—anything that represents something other than itself. *Symbols* can be found in everyday life as well as in literature.

EXAMPLES:

1. The skull-and-crossbones is a symbol for pirates or poison
2. The American flag, the Stars-and-Stripes, is a symbol for the United States of America
3. The elephant and the donkey are symbols for the Republican Party and the Democratic Party, respectively.

NOTE: Some of the finest uses of symbols in English literature can be found in the poetry of the 18th-century poet-painter William Blake.

synecdoche—any type of expression that describes a person or a thing as if it were only a part of the whole person or thing.

EXAMPLES of *synecdoche*:

1. We refer to our car as our "wheels" because the wheels are an important part of the whole car

2. If you take dangerous risks, we say that you "risk your neck" because, obviously, your neck is an important part of your whole body.

KEEP IN MIND: Synecdoche is a figure of speech.

theme—the point of a story. For example, Shakespeare's sonnets are about love; however, the point of each sonnet, or its *theme*, is different: the point of one sonnet might be "Love does not last," yet the point of another sonnet might be "Love is sometimes painful." In a work of literature, there may be more than one theme, and the theme (or themes) may or may not be directly stated.

CAUTION: Theme is *not* plot. In the novel *Moby Dick*, for example, the plot concerns one man's pursuit of a giant white whale; however, the theme, or the point of the story, might be "Revenge can be self-destructive."

KEEP IN MIND: *Theme analysis* is a type of *critical writing* in which the theme of a work of literature is both identified and discussed in terms of the author's development of that theme. Usually readers agree on the plot of a work of literature but may disagree on the theme (or themes) of a work of literature.

tone—the attitude that an author gives to a work of literature. There are many ways to describe *tone*, such as angry, cynical, devotional, sarcastic, and serious.

tragedy—traditionally a type of drama in which the tragic hero or heroine, the main character who is basically a good person of high position, is ruined or destroyed because of his or her own misjudgment (tragic flaw); this error in judgment is usually due to a fatal weakness in his or her character. Because that error is not recognized until it is too late (after his or her downfall), that character, in the end, must suffer and die. For example, in Shakespeare's *Macbeth*, because of his overambition, Macbeth misjudges the witches' prophecies and in so doing brings about his tragic suffering and death. Famous *tragedies* include the ancient Greek Sophocles's *Oedipus Rex*, his contemporary Aeschylus's *Oresteia*, and Shakespeare's *Romeo and Juliet*, *Julius Caesar*, *Macbeth*, *Hamlet*, and *King Lear*.

CAUTION: This definition of tragedy is one based upon the ancient Greek philosopher Aristotle's. Modern definitions of tragedy will vary, as in the 20th-century American playwright Arthur Miller's portrayal of tragedy in his *Death of a Salesman*.

unities—the time, place, and action that occur in a play. The *unities* were adapted from the ancient Greek philosopher Aristotle's ideas about drama. These unities require that a play occur in one day in one place and have one action. NOTE: A play is not required to follow Aristotle's unities.

II.
Composition—
the *craft* of written communication

argumentation (argumentative writing)—an attempt to persuade the reader that one side of an issue is better than
any other side of that issue. The first step in *argumentation* is to choose one side of an issue. The second step is
to word very carefully a position on that issue. Next,
evidence must be found both for and against that position. Evidence for that position must be proved strong,
and evidence against must be proved weak. In this way,
even the opposing evidence is used to an advantage.
TIP: For the greatest advantage in *argumentative writing*,
begin with the least convincing reasons and build
up to the most convincing reasons.
EXAMPLE: The Declaration of Independence.
KEEP IN MIND: Argumentation is one of the four types
of writing (or discourse): argumentation, description, exposition, and narration.

audience—the person or persons for whom a written work is
intended. Before a writer begins to write, he or she
usually identifies the *audience* for whom the work is
intended and considers that audience's background (age,
education, knowledge of the topic, vocabulary, etc.).

TIP: When a student writes a paper for a class, his or her audience will often be identified by the teacher; otherwise, the audience will be the teacher and/or the writer's classmates.

bibliography—the list of references (articles, books, interviews, etc.) that a writer used as sources of information. A *bibliography* is alphabetized by the authors' last names and is included at the end of a work. Because the form for each type of bibliographic entry is different (for example, the form for a book is different from that for a magazine article or an interview), be sure to refer to the style sheet or handbook that your teacher recommends. The following cites this book as a sample entry:

> Malless, Stan, and Jeff McQuain. *The Elements of English: A Glossary of Basic Terms for Literature, Composition, and Grammar*. Lanham, Md.: Madison Books, 1988.

NOTE: When a writer wants to list all the references that he or she consulted, including those not referred to in the text, the bibliography may be labeled "Works Consulted," as was done for this book.

cause-and-effect writing—an attempt to show the reader how and why one thing (a cause) leads to another thing (an effect) or why one thing (an effect) follows from another thing (a cause). In *cause-and-effect writing*, a writer first identifies something that leads to or follows from something else. Once that cause or that effect has been identified, the writer then identifies the other half of the cause-and-effect connection. The final step is to prove that those things are, in fact, connected.

DANGER: Do not assume that knowing an effect means automatically knowing its cause. (A bomb can cause a loud noise, but a loud noise is not necessarily caused by a bomb.) Also, do not oversimplify: the most recent cause is not necessarily the only cause.

(An injury near the site of a bomb-blast is not necessarily caused by that bomb-blast.)

classification writing—an attempt to tell the reader why
something is in one group and not in another group. In
classification writing, you must decide how to divide a big
group of things into smaller groups. Usually each smaller
group is made up of things that are similar to each other
and yet different from the rest of the bigger group. In
other words, the aim of classification writing is first to
find similarities and differences in a group of things, so
that you can then create smaller groups according to
those similarities and differences.
>EXAMPLE: All of the students at your school belong to
one big group: the student body. That big group can
be divided into smaller groups—for instance, freshmen, sophomores, juniors, and seniors. Each
smaller group is made up of students who are similar to each other and yet different from the rest of
the big group.

coherence—the unity that is created when there is a clearly
logical sequence of ideas. A well-written sentence, paragraph, or essay must have *coherence*.
>EXAMPLE: The following sentence lacks coherence:
"She got wet, and it rained on Tuesday." One way
to improve the coherence of that sentence might be
"Because it rained on Tuesday, she got wet." Why is
this sentence coherent? The idea that "She got wet"
on Tuesday is given unity because the logic of the
sentence has been developed clearly: "Because it
rained. . . ."

comparison/contrast writing—an attempt to show how two
or more things are similar (comparison) and/or how
those things are different (contrast). *Comparison/contrast
writing* can be organized in at least two ways: a writer
can choose to discuss all of the similarities first and then

discuss all of the differences, or he or she can choose to discuss one similarity, then one difference, then another similarity, and so on.

conclusion (concluding sentence/concluding paragraph)—a statement on which the writer ends the discussion of a topic. A good *conclusion* not only will remind the reader of a topic's main points but also will do so with imagination and an understanding of the topic.
CAUTION: In your conclusion, do *not* simply repeat your topic sentence.
EXAMPLE: Lincoln's *Gettysburg Address*, which concludes, ". . . that government of the people, by the people, for the people, shall not perish from the earth."

conferencing (writing conference)—a technique for improving writing. *Conferencing* involves the discussing of one's writing with another person (peer, parent, teacher), with others (group), or alone as one's own critic (self). In the writing process, conferencing for content occurs during the drafting and revision stages. Proofreading conferences usually occur after content has been set and before the final draft is written.
NOTE: Conferencing can be a part of a *writing workshop*, which allows the writer time in class to write, to share his or her writing, to receive helpful responses, and to respond to the writing of others.

connotation—whatever a word suggests beyond its dictionary definition. For example, sun is defined in the dictionary as "the star around which the earth revolves." The *connotations* of sun, however, might include warmth, life, happiness, and so on.

critique—a French word used as a noun (a review of a particular work) and as a verb (the act of reviewing). A *critique* of a literary work (or student writing assignment) involves both a close reading and a critical analysis of that work for the purpose of identifying its strengths as well as offering suggestions for its improvement.

HINT: The review of a play or of a film is a type of critique.

definition writing—an attempt to state the meaning of either a thing or an idea. The first step in *definition writing* involves classification: a writer tries to determine the group to which that thing or idea belongs. (Football, for example, belongs to the group of things called sports.) The next step is to show how that thing or idea differs from the other members of its group. (Although football and softball are both called sports, for example, they are different in many ways.) Determining what something is not can lead to a definition of what that something is.

KEEP IN MIND: There are two types of definition writing: *concrete definition* (the definition of an object) and *abstract definition* (the definition of an idea).

denotation—whatever a word means according to its dictionary definition. For example, sun is defined in the dictionary as "the star around which the earth revolves." That definition is the *denotation* of sun.

HINT: Both d̲enotation and d̲ictionary begin with the letter d̲.

description (descriptive writing)—an attempt to recreate for the reader a person, place, or thing as if that recreating were a painting drawn with words. Unlike a painting, however, *description* is not limited to just the sense of sight; it appeals to our other senses as well. For example, the writer describes sounds, tastes, smells, and feelings, using details, metaphors, and images to recreate his or her unique point of view (place and attitude).

EXAMPLE: Edgar Allan Poe's "Tales and Sketches," especially "The Island of the Fay" and "Landor's Cottage."

KEEP IN MIND: Description is one of the four types of writing (or discourse): argumentation, description, exposition, and narration.

diction—a writer's choice of words. A good writer knows that *diction* must be appropriate to the subject and purpose of his or her writing. In formal writing, for instance, the use of *cliches* (overused words or worn-out expressions such as "busy as a bee") or *slang* (words that have developed various informal meanings such as "cool," "creep," "freak," "nerd," and "weirdo") would be considered trite or inappropriate diction; however, cliches and slang might be considered appropriate diction in informal writing.

NOTE: Diction also refers to speech.

editing—the deleting and/or rearranging (by the writer or an editor) of parts of a piece of writing. *Editing* does not usually involve the actual rewriting of a text.

essay—a composition in which a writer explores a single idea in one or more paragraphs. An *essay* can be either informal (personal) or formal. In an *informal* essay, the writer expresses personal ideas for their own sake. In a *formal* essay (exposition), on the other hand, a writer expresses ideas for the sake of an audience.

TIP: Your teacher may refer to an essay as a *theme* or as a *composition*.

exposition (expository writing)—an attempt to inform, instruct, or explain to the reader.

NOTE: *Exposition* is usually considered formal writing.

KEEP IN MIND: Exposition is one of the four types of writing (or discourse): argumentation, description, exposition, and narration.

final draft—the end product of a piece of writing that has gone through the whole process of drafting, revising, and polishing. A *final draft* should reflect the writer's best efforts at content, mechanics, and neatness.

TIP: A final draft is often double-spaced, is written or typed on one side of the page, and always should be titled.

focus—a term used to describe the central reason for a piece of writing. *Focus* is used as a noun: a writer's focus is on the centermost idea of a paragraph or of an entire piece of writing, like the sun in its solar system. Focus is also used as a verb: the writer must focus the topic by asking himself or herself questions such as "What is important about this?" or "What is this really about?"

NOTE: Once the focus has been determined, it should be given more space than those points of lesser importance that revolve around it.

footnote—a reference to a specific source of factual or quoted information that tells the reader where that information was found. Currently there are two techniques for *footnotes*:

1. *numbered*—the entry appears either at the bottom of the page on which the reference is cited or as an *endnote* on a separate page at the end of the text. The number of the footnote corresponds to the same number found at the end of and slightly above the information cited in the body of the text.[1] For example, a footnote for the above information would look like this:

[1]Stan Malless and Jeff McQuain, *The Elements of English: A Glossary of Basic Terms for Literature, Composition, and Grammar* (Lanham, Md.: University Press of America, 1988), p.33.

CAUTION: The form for numbered footnotes varies: The form for a book is different from the form for a magazine article or an interview, and so on. Be sure to refer to the style sheet or handbook that your teacher recommends.
2. *parenthetical* (or in-text)—the entry appears in parentheses immediately after the information to which it refers. This type of referencing usually requires only the author's name and the page number(s) from which the work was cited. The additional information is included in a bibliography at the end of the text. For example, a parenthetical note for the above information would look like this: (Malless, McQuain, 34).

non sequitur—a Latin phrase that means "it does not follow." A *non sequitur* is a mistake that a writer makes; it is an unintentional, illogical shift from one idea to another idea. Usually a non sequitur is a sentence that does not follow logically the sentence(s) before it. Take, for example, the following group of sentences:

"Martin Luther King, Jr., delivered his 'I Have a Dream' speech on August 28, 1963. A quarter of a million people were in Washington, D.C., to hear it. Many students visit Washington, D.C., every year."

The final sentence is a non sequitur because it does not follow logically the sentences before it.

paragraph—an organized and coherent group of sentences that develops one main idea. In narrative, descriptive, and informal writing, a new *paragraph* may indicate a change in time, place, action, or speaker. In formal argumentative and expository writing, a paragraph has a beginning (topic sentence), a middle (development of the topic), and an end (concluding sentence), and these three parts should be clearly related to one another.

parallel structure—the repetition of the same type of word, phrase, or clause. *Parallel structure* (or *parallelism*) is an effective way to give balance to a sentence. Take, for example, the following sentence: "She likes dancing, to sing, and jogging." Note that *to sing* is not the same type of word as *dancing* and *jogging*; therefore, that sentence does not have parallel structure. One way to correct that sentence would be "She likes dancing, *singing*, and jogging."

EXAMPLES of parallelism:
1. parallel phrases:
   ". . . of the people, by the people, for the people"
2. parallel clauses:
   "I came; I saw; I conquered."

plagiarism—the unethical use of someone else's original work. Specifically, plagiarism involves the use of another person's original ideas, research, or exact words without giving the proper credit to that person. To avoid *plagiarism* when you use someone else's work in your writing, always give credit to that person's work. Use quotation marks and/or footnotes to show that the information has been borrowed.

DANGER: A plagiarist can be prosecuted by law.

precis—an accurate and precise condensation of a written work. The *precis* maintains the original author's point of view and is a carefully condensed version of that work.

CAUTION: Do not confuse precis with paraphrase or with summary. A *paraphrase* is a restatement in different words of a written work or part of a written work; however, it is not a condensation of that work. A *summary* is a brief version of the main ideas in a piece of writing.

WARNING: When writing an analysis of a work of literature, do not confuse analysis with *plot summary* (simply retelling the main events in the plot of a story).

prewriting—the earliest stage in the writing process. *Prewriting* is the informal sketching or thinking through ("rehearsing") of ideas the writer has about a topic.

process (or "how to") writing—an attempt to tell the reader how to do something. In *process writing*, the writer must first be knowledgeable about the process that he or she is going to explain. Once the writer feels confident about the process, he or she should list the necessary steps in the procedure, making sure that those steps are in order and that no steps are missing. Finally, the writer should very carefully word the instructions for each step, making sure to use words the reader can understand.
NOTE: The consideration of audience is especially important for process writing.
TIP: A basic example of process writing is any recipe in a cookbook.

proofreading—the last stage in the writing process before the final draft is submitted. *Proofreading* is the close reading of a text for the purpose of finding and correcting errors in *mechanics* (spelling, punctuation, grammar, usage, and typing/handwriting) rather than in *content* (the ideas and the arrangement of those ideas).

redundancy—the unnecessary repetition of words, facts, or ideas. Take, for example, the following sentence: "She is a famous and well-known poet who writes poetry." The unnecessary repetition of "famous" and "well-known" is a *redundancy*, as is the repetition of the obvious fact that a "poet" is one who "writes poetry."
TIP: The word "redundancy" or "redundant" comes from a Latin root *unda* that means "wave-like," as in the repeating nature of ocean waves.

research paper—a multi-paragraph essay in which a writer provides information or presents evidence to prove a thesis and, depending upon the assignment, will use footnotes and a bibliography to refer to the primary or secondary sources for that information or evidence. A *primary source* is the document or object being studied. For example, in a *research paper* about Mark Twain's 19th-century novel *Huckleberry Finn*, the primary source would be the novel itself. A *secondary source*, on the other hand, is a work already written about the document or object being studied. In that research paper about *Huckleberry Finn*, for example, a secondary source might be a biography of Mark Twain (Samuel Clemens).

revising—the process of rewriting. Experienced writers know that *revising* is inescapable. They expect to rewrite or change single words, phrases, sentences, thesis statements, and paragraphs many times in a piece of writing before its content is set. Once that content is set, the writer proofreads and edits (or "polishes") before writing the final draft.

rhetoric—the art or artistry of persuasion. In ancient Greece, a "rhetor" was a public speaker who had been trained how to persuade an audience. In a modern "composition and rhetoric" class, *rhetoric* still means, roughly, what it did for the Greeks: the ways that one verbally can shape reality.
BEWARE: A popular meaning of "rhetoric" is artful communication that is more art than communication.

rhetorical question—asking a question without expecting an answer. A writer (or speaker) does not expect an answer to a *rhetorical question* because he or she already knows the answer; the question is asked to draw attention to what is, in the author's mind, the only answer.
EXAMPLE: "What's this world coming to?"
CAUTION: A writer should not overuse the rhetorical question.

rough draft (first draft)—the writer's first attempts to get ideas on paper. *Rough drafts* range from the totally unorganized to sentences and paragraphs that are fairly well organized. Many experienced writers will double-space first drafts and write on only one side of the page in order to leave room for their revisions.

   TIP: Content is the most important consideration in writing and revising the rough draft. Until the content is set, attention to mechanics may be minimal.

style—the "personality" of a piece of writing. That personality is a mixture of the individual ways an author uses language. Although a writer's *style* is practically impossible to define, there are a number of specific elements contributing to that style. Among the most common of these elements are diction, figures of speech, frequency of grammatical patterns, sentence type and length, and use of imagery.

syntax—the principle of language that makes communication meaningful. In a composition, problems of *syntax* usually involve problems of word order. Take, for example, the following sentence: "To Wanda threw Bob the ball." Note that syntax needs to be improved in that sentence to make communication more meaningful. To improve syntax, arrange the words differently. For instance, one arrangement would be "Bob threw the ball to Wanda."

thesaurus—a book that is similar to a dictionary but, instead of defining any given word, offers a list of other words similar in meaning (synonyms) to that given word.

   TIP: To avoid using any word too often, a writer uses a *thesaurus* to find other words that are similar in meaning to that word.

thesis statement—the specific sentence in a written composition that states what the writer will attempt to prove in that composition. In formal writing, the *thesis* is usually stated in the introductory paragraph and is the topic sentence for that paragraph.

TIP: The word "thesis" comes from the ancient Greek root that means "to take a position" and is also found in such words as "hypothesis," "antithesis," and "synthesis."

topic sentence—the specific sentence in a paragraph that states the one main idea that the writer will focus on and develop in that paragraph. The *topic sentence* is almost always the first sentence in a paragraph.

transition (connective)—specific word, phrase, or clause that closes the gap between sentences or ideas in a written work.

EXAMPLE:

Transitions are also known as *connectives* because they connect one sentence or idea to another sentence or idea. A transition can be as simple as a word or a phrase. For example, the phrase "for example" is a transition, because it helps close the gap between the previous sentence and this one.

To close the gap between two paragraphs, a transition should connect the concluding sentence of one paragraph to the topic sentence of the next. This connection can be made by repeating a key word or phrase. For instance, the topic sentence of this paragraph repeats a key phrase from the concluding sentence of the previous paragraph: "close the gap."

unity—the effect created when all the parts of a paragraph or a composition are relevant to the whole paragraph or composition. For example, the *unity* of a paragraph or a composition occurs when the body and the conclusion are relevant to the thesis statement or main idea of that paragraph or composition.

III.

Grammar—
the *rules* of written communication
(*and* spoken communication)

active voice/passive voice—the way that a verb transmits
action between the subject and the object in a sentence.
The writer uses *active voice* when the verb transmits
action directly from the subject to the object; for example,
in "Lightning strikes trees," the verb ("strikes") transmits action directly from the subject ("Lightning") to the
object ("trees"). In contrast, *passive voice* is used by the
writer when the verb transmits action *in*directly, as in
"Trees are struck by lightning." The writer uses passive
voice to emphasize what would normally be the object of
a sentence: the object becomes the subject of that sentence.
TIP: Avoid using passive voice in writing. Active voice
makes your words more forceful.
WARNING: Do not confuse *passive voice* with *past tense*.

adjective—a word that adds detail to a noun or a pronoun.
For example, in "The woman laughed," the writer can
add detail to the noun "woman" by using an *adjective*:

41

"The young woman laughed." Although usually a single word, an adjective can also be the following:

1. infinitive phrase: "She had the urge *to laugh*"
2. participial phrase: "I heard the woman *laughing behind me*"
3. prepositional phrase: "The woman *behind me* laughed"
4. clause: "I heard the woman *who was laughing behind me.*"

NOTE: The *articles* "a," "an," and "the" are used as adjectives. "The" is a *definite article* because it is specific ("the book"); "a" and "an" are *indefinite articles* because they do not specify ("a book," "an apple").

KEEP IN MIND: An adjective is one of the parts of speech.

adverb—a word that adds detail to the action of a verb. In "She laughed," for example, the writer can add detail to the verb's action by using an *adverb*: "She laughed *nervously*." An adverb can also add detail to an adjective ("*very* funny") as well as to another adverb ("*very* slowly"). Although usually a single word, an adverb can also be the following:

1. an infinitive phrase: "She tried hard *to laugh*"
2. a prepositional phrase "She shook *with laughter*"
3. a clause: "*Whenever she laughed*, she shook."

CAUTION: Most adverbs end in -*ly*, but easily overlooked words like *not* and *very* are also adverbs.

KEEP IN MIND: An adverb is one of the parts of speech.

agreement—the correct use of number and gender. There are two basic types of *agreement*:

1. *pronoun/antecedent*—a pronoun must agree in number (either singular or plural) and in gender (masculine, feminine, or neuter) with the antecedent that it renames. The *antecedent* is the noun or pronoun to which the later pronoun refers and almost always comes before the later pronoun. For example, in the sentence "Each student takes

courses they want to take," notice that the plural pronoun "they" does not agree in number with the singular antecedent "Each student." In order to have pronoun/antecedent agreement, one way to correct that sentence would be "Each student takes courses that he or she wants to take."

2. *subject/verb*—a verb must agree in number with its subject. A singular subject takes a singular verb ("He laughs"); a plural subject takes a plural verb ("They laugh").

appositive—a word or phrase that immediately follows a noun and has the same meaning as that noun.

EXAMPLES of *appositives*:

1. a one-word appositive: "Their dog *Captain* howls all night"
2. an appositive phrase: "Their dog, *an old collie,* howls all night."

HINT: An appositive phrase always includes a noun and usually begins with "a," "an," or "the."

clause—any group of words that includes both a subject *and* a verb (predicate).

NOTE: The two types of *clause* are *dependent (subordinate) clause* and *independent (main) clause.*

comparative adjective/superlative adjective—a word that compares two or more nouns that share the same quality (size, distance, speed, etc.).

A *comparative adjective* compares *two* nouns in terms of "more" or "less" (as in "Jupiter is *bigger* than Earth").

A *superlative adjective* compares *three or more* nouns in terms of "most" or "least" (as in "Of the nine planets, Jupiter is the *biggest*").

HINT: Comparative adjectives usually end in *-er*; superlative adjectives usually end in *-est.*

complement—any word or words that normally follow both the subject and the verb to complete the meaning of a sentence. A *complement* can be a direct object, an indirect object, a predicate adjective, or a predicate nominative.
TIP: A complement completes.

complex sentence—any sentence that combines one independent clause and at least one dependent clause.
EXAMPLE of a *complex sentence*: "When you read this sentence, you are reading a complex sentence." The complex sentence combines a dependent clause ("When you read this sentence") and an independent clause ("you are reading a complex sentence").
THINK OF IT THIS WAY:
complex sentence = 1 dependent clause + 1 independent clause.

compound sentence—any sentence in which two or more independent clauses are joined by a conjunction.
EXAMPLE of a *compound sentence*: "You are reading one independent clause, and now you are reading another independent clause." The conjunction ("and") joins those two independent clauses to make a compound sentence.
THINK OF IT THIS WAY:
compound sentence = 1 independent clause + 1 conjunction + 1 independent clause.

compound-complex sentence—any sentence that combines at least one independent clause and one complex sentence.
EXAMPLE of a *compound-complex sentence*: "When you begin with a dependent clause, you add one independent clause to make a complex sentence, and adding another independent clause makes this sentence a compound-complex sentence."
THINK OF IT THIS WAY:

compound-complex sentence = 1 independent clause + 1 complex sentence.

conjunction (coordinating/subordinating)—a word that connects words, phrases, or clauses.

The *coordinating conjunctions* include the following: "and," "but," "for," "nor," "or," "so," "yet." These conjunctions join words or phrases as well as clauses; in fact, a coordinating conjunction connects two clauses without making either clause more important than the other (*coordination*).

TIP: When a coordinating conjunction connects two independent clauses, a comma is usually placed before that conjunction.

The *subordinating conjunctions* include the following: "as," "because," "since," "until," "when," "which," "while," "who," etc. These conjunctions begin subordinate (dependent) clauses and make those clauses less important than the main clause (*subordination*).

KEEP IN MIND: A conjunction is one of the parts of speech.

dangling modifier—in a sentence, any modifier (adjective or adverb) that does not have someone or something to describe. A *dangling modifier* can be a single word, a phrase, or a clause and is said to "dangle" when its sentence lacks the someone or something that the modifier is supposed to be describing.

EXAMPLE: "Before writing a composition, the audience should be considered." In that sentence, "Before writing a composition" is a dangling modifier because the sentence lacks the someone or something that is writing the composition. (It reads as if the audience were writing the composition.) One way to correct that sentence would be to rewrite it as the following: "Before a student begins to write a composition, he or she should consider its audience."

HINT: When a dangling modifier occurs, it often either begins with or includes a word ending in *-ing* and is usually found at the beginning of a sentence.

dependent (subordinate) clause—any group of words that includes both a subject *and* a verb but cannot be a complete sentence. A *dependent clause* "depends" on more information to complete the sentence. Take, for example, the following sentence: "When the sun sets, the lion roars." The dependent clause in that sentence is "When the sun sets" because it includes both a subject ("sun") *and* a verb ("sets") but needs more information to be a complete sentence.
REMINDER: There are three types of dependent clauses:
1. an adjective clause: "The bucket *that he kicked* was empty"
2. an adverb clause: "*When he kicked the bucket*, it was empty"
3. a noun clause: "He kicked *what was an empty bucket*."

direct object—in a sentence, the noun or pronoun to which the action of the verb in that sentence is directed. A *direct object* can be a single word, a phrase, or a clause.
EXAMPLES:
1. direct object as noun: "He kicked the *bucket*"
2. direct object as pronoun: "He kicked *it*"
3. direct object as phrase: "He liked *to kick the bucket*"
4. direct object as clause: "He kicked *what was in the bucket*."
RULE: Direct objects follow only action verbs.
KEEP IN MIND: A direct object is a complement.

gerund—any noun that ends in *-ing* and is verb-like in form. A *gerund* can be the subject, the object, or the predicate nominative, but never the verb of a sentence. Take, for example, the following sentence: "Smoking is dangerous

to your health." The gerund "smoking," which is the subject of that sentence, ends in -*ing* and is verb-like in form (that is, it is formed from the verb "to smoke").
KEEP IN MIND:
1. A gerund is a verbal.
2. A gerund phrase usually begins with a gerund.

independent (main) clause—any group of words that combines a subject *and* a verb to make a sentence. In fact, an *independent clause* by itself *is* a sentence.
NOTICE: An independent clause can be as short as two words ("They laughed") or even as short as one word ("Help!") when the subject "You" is understood.

indirect object—in a sentence, the noun or pronoun (the person or thing) that receives the direct object. Any sentence that contains an *indirect object* must also contain a direct object. Take, for example, the following sentence: "The horror movie gave them nightmares." In that sentence, "them" is the indirect object because it is receiving the direct object ("nightmares").
KEEP IN MIND: An indirect object is a complement.

infinitive—*to* followed by the simplest form of a verb. An *infinitive* can be a noun, an adjective, or an adverb.
EXAMPLES:
1. infinitive as noun: "*To laugh* helps"
2. infinitive as adjective: "The ability *to laugh* helps"
3. infinitive as adverb: "She was ready *to laugh*."
KEEP IN MIND: An infinitive is a verbal.
NOTE: Sometimes the infinitive is more than one word, as in "to have been caught" or "to have laughed."

interjection—the part of speech that, when used in a sentence, does not relate grammatically to the other words in that sentence. An *interjection* is usually an expression of emotion or surprise. Take, for example, the following

sentence: "Wow, my head hurts!" The word "wow" is an interjection because it expresses emotion and does not relate grammatically to the other words in that sentence.
KEEP IN MIND: An interjection is one of the parts of speech.

linking verb—any verb that does not transmit action. Instead, a *linking verb* works, in some ways, as an equal sign (=) does: what comes before the linking verb is *equal to* what comes after the linking verb.
EXAMPLE: "Earth is a planet." In that sentence, "is" is a linking verb because what comes before it (the noun "Earth") is equal to what comes after it (the noun "planet").
Also, what comes before a linking verb can be *described by* what comes after the linking verb.
EXAMPLES:
1. "The moon was full." In this sentence, the verb "was" is a linking verb because what comes before it (the noun "moon") is described by what comes after it (the adjective "full").
2. "The planets are in orbit." In this sentence, the noun "planets" is described by the adverb phrase "in orbit."
NOTE: The most common linking verb is any form of the verb "to be" ("is," "are," "was," "were," "has been," "had been," "would be," "will be," "will have been," etc.). Other linking verbs involve the senses ("The rose *smells* sweet") and feelings ("She *feels* relieved").

misplaced modifier—in a sentence, any modifier (adjective or adverb) that, by its placement, seems to describe one person or thing but should actually be describing another person or thing in that sentence. A *misplaced modifier* can be a single word, a phrase, or a clause. To correct a misplaced modifier, simply move the modifier closer to what it should be modifying.

EXAMPLE: "A writer should consider his or her audience when writing a paper." In that sentence, "when writing a paper" is a misplaced modifier because "A writer," not "his or her audience," is "writing a paper." One way to correct the sentence is to rewrite it as the following: "When writing a paper, a writer should consider his or her audience."

TIP: A misplaced modifier differs from a dangling modifier in that a dangling modifier has nothing in the sentence to modify.

noun—a word that identifies a person, a place, or a thing. A *noun* can be a single word, a phrase (gerund or infinitive), or a clause.
EXAMPLES:
1. noun as single word: *"Laughter* is fun"
2. noun as phrase:
   gerund phrase: *"Laughing out loud* is fun"
   infinitive phrase: *"To laugh out loud* is fun"
3. noun as clause: *"Whoever laughs out loud* has fun."

KEEP IN MIND: A noun is one of the parts of speech.

participle—any adjective that is verb-like in form and that usually ends in *-ing, -ed, -en,* or *-t.* A *participle* can be either a *present* participle (ending in *-ing*) or a *past* participle (ending usually in *-ed, -en,* or *-t*).
EXAMPLES:
1. *"Shooting* stars fell at night" ("shoot*ing*" as present participle)
2. "The *exhausted* boxer collapsed" ("exhaust*ed*" as past participle)
3. "The *broken* mirror brought bad luck ("brok*en*" as past participle)
4. "The roof of the *burnt* house collapsed" ("burn*t*" as past participle).

KEEP IN MIND:
  1. A participle is a verbal.
  2. A participial phrase usually begins with a partici-
     ple.

parts of speech—the eight basic types of words. These eight
  parts of speech are the following: noun, pronoun, verb,
  adjective, adverb, preposition, conjunction, interjection.

phrase—any group of words that lacks either a subject or a
  verb or both. Most often the type of *phrase* being used is
  determined by the first word or words in the phrase.
  There are several types of phrase:
  1. A *prepositional phrase* begins with a preposition ("He
     ran *down the street*")
  2. A *verb phrase* begins with a verb ("He *is running*")
  3. A *participial phrase* begins with a participle ("*Running
     down the street*, he screamed for help")
  4. A *gerund phrase* begins with a gerund ("*Laughing out
     loud* is fun")
  5. An *infinitive phrase* begins with an infinitive ("*To laugh
     out loud* is fun")
  6. An *appositive phrase* usually begins with "a," "an," or
     "the" ("The boy, *a good runner*, raced down the
     street").

predicate—everything in a sentence but the subject of that
  sentence. A *predicate* either tells what its subject is doing
  or gives more information about its subject. In the previous sentence, for example, everything after the word
  "predicate" is the predicate of that sentence.

predicate adjective—any adjective that follows a linking verb
  ("is," "was," "were," "has been," "seems," etc.) and
  describes the subject of its sentence. Take, for example,
  the following sentence: "The moon is full." In that sentence, the word "full" is the *predicate adjective* because it

follows the linking verb ("is") and describes the subject ("moon").

KEEP IN MIND: A predicate adjective is a complement.

predicate nominative—any noun or pronoun that follows a linking verb ("is," "was," "were," "has been," "seems," etc.) and is equal to the subject of its sentence. Take, for example, the following sentence: "That planet is Mars." In that sentence, the noun "Mars" is the *predicate nominative* because it follows the linking verb ("is") and is equal to the subject ("planet").

KEEP IN MIND: A predicate nominative is a complement.

preposition—a word that describes the position of someone or something in relation to someone or something else. Take, for example, the following sentence: "The baby is in the crib." In that sentence, the word "in" is a *preposition* because it describes the position ("in") of someone ("baby") in relation to something else ("crib").

EXAMPLES of prepositions: "about," "around," "at," "between," "by," "down," "for," "from," "in," "of," "out," "over," "to," "under," "with," etc.

CLUE: "Position" is in the word "pre*position.*"

NOTE: The "position" that a preposition describes does not necessarily mean a physical position; for example, the preposition "by" in "The play was written *by* Shakespeare" is not a physical position but shows the position of the play in relation to its author, Shakespeare.

KEEP IN MIND:

1. A preposition is one of the parts of speech.
2. A prepositional phrase begins with a preposition.

pronoun—a word that can replace a noun. There are seven kinds of *pronouns:*

1. *personal*—I, you, he, him, she, her, it, we, us, they, them
2. *possessive*—my, mine, your, yours, its, his, her, hers, our, ours, their, theirs
3. *reflexive*—myself, yourself, himself, herself, itself, ourselves, yourselves, themselves
4. *relative*—who, whom, which, that, whose
5. *interrogative*—who, whom, which, what, whose
6. *demonstrative*—this, that, these, those
7. *indefinite*—among the most common are the following: all, each, anyone, both, few, many, most, none, one, some, someone.

KEEP IN MIND: A pronoun is one of the parts of speech.

pronoun reference—the rule that any pronoun having an antecedent (the noun or pronoun to which that pronoun refers) must always refer *clearly* to that antecedent. For clear *pronoun reference*, keep the pronoun and its antecedent as close together as possible.

EXAMPLE: In the sentence "The sheriff saw the outlaw after he went to town," notice that the pronoun "he" does not refer clearly to the antecedent; in fact, its antecedent could be either "sheriff" or "outlaw." One way to correct that sentence would be "After the sheriff went to town, he saw the outlaw." Another way to correct that sentence would be "After the outlaw went to town, he saw the sheriff."

run-on sentence—an error in which two or more sentences either are joined by a comma or have *no* punctuation mark between them.

BEWARE: A *run-on sentence* can be very short: "She laughed, he cried."

NOTE: There are at least three ways to correct a run-on sentence:

1. Use a period: "She laughed. He cried."
2. Use a semicolon: "She laughed; he cried."

3. Use a conjunction after a comma: "She laughed, but he cried."

sentence fragment—an error in which either a phrase or a dependent clause is followed by an end mark of punctuation (usually a period).
EXAMPLES of *sentence fragments*:
1. phrase as sentence fragment: "Singing in the rain."
2. dependent clause as sentence fragment: "When he was singing in the rain."
REMINDER: Neither a phrase nor a dependent clause can stand alone as a sentence.

shift (in tense/in person)—any error that involves an unnecessary change in tense or in person. Either type of *shift* should be avoided in formal writing.
A *shift in tense* is an unnecessary change from one verb tense to another verb tense. Take, for example, the following sentence: "She laughs out loud and then smiled." In that sentence, there is an unnecessary shift from present tense ("laughs") to past tense ("smiled"). One way to correct this shift in tense would be "She laughs out loud and then smiles."
A *shift in person* is an unnecessary change from one pronoun to another pronoun. Take, for example, the following sentence: "One gets a driver's license after you pass a test." In that sentence, there is an unnecessary shift in person from one pronoun ("one") to another pronoun ("you"). One way to correct this shift in person would be "You get a driver's license after you pass a test."

simple sentence—any word or group of words that combines a single (simple) subject *and* a single (simple) verb to make a complete thought. A *simple sentence* can be as short as two words ("He laughed") or even as short as one word ("Help!") in which the subject "You" is understood.

REMINDER: A simple sentence is an independent clause.

tense—the form of a verb that shows time. The three times that a *tense* can show are *past, present,* and *future*: "They forgot," "They forget," and "They will forget." In addition to these three simple tenses, there are three perfect tenses, each needing helping verbs: *past perfect* ("They had forgotten"), *present perfect* ("They have forgotten"), and *future perfect* ("They will have forgotten").

WARNING: Do not shift from one tense to another without reason. For example, "The phone rang, and I answer it" should be either "The phone rings, and I answer it" or "The phone rang, and I answered it."

verb—a word that tells what someone or something (the *subject*) does or is. A *verb* can be either a single word or a phrase and will belong to one of two groups:

    1. *action verbs*—tell what someone or something does. An action verb that takes a direct object is called a *transitive verb* ("She reads books"); an action verb that does not take a direct object is called an *intransitive verb* ("She laughs").

    2. *linking verbs* - tell what someone or something is ("The moon is full"). A linking verb, which never takes a direct object, is also called intransitive.

A *verb phrase,* which consists of two or more words, includes at least one *helping (auxiliary) verb* such as "has," "can," "would," "might," or "must," as in the sentence "I must be going."

TIP: Action verbs take direct objects and indirect objects; linking verbs take predicate nominatives and predicate adjectives. (Sometimes a linking verb is followed by an adverb.)

KEEP IN MIND: A verb is one of the parts of speech.

verbal—gerund, participle (present and past), or infinitive. A *verbal*, as its name suggests, is verb-like in form, but it is not used as a verb. Instead, it can be a gerund (noun), a participle (adjective), or an infinitive (noun, adjective, adverb).

EXAMPLES of verbals:

1. gerund: "*Smoking* is dangerous to your health" ("*Smoking*" as gerund).
2. participle: "*Shooting* stars fell all night" ("*Shooting*" as present participle). "The *exhausted* boxer collapsed" ("*exhausted*" as past participle).
3. infinitive: "*To laugh* helps" (noun). "The ability *to laugh* helps" (adjective). "She was ready *to laugh*" (adverb).

Capitalization

AUTHORS' NOTE: The following "rules" for capitalization and punctuation are not absolutes; they vary with each writer and usage handbook. There are, of course, additional rules for capitalization and for marks of punctuation. Those that we have listed below are the ones we have found to be the most common in student writing.

Capitalize
1. the first letter of a sentence
2. proper nouns (names that are not used to describe common, everyday things). For example, "White House" is capitalized when it refers to the home of the President of the United States but is not capitalized when it is used to describe any common, everyday white house
3. adjectives derived from proper nouns (American from America, etc.)
4. the first letter of a direct quotation (Patrick Henry said, "Give me liberty or give me death!")
5. the first letter of a title and the first letter of each word in that title except for articles, conjunctions, and prepositions of fewer than five letters (*The Catcher in the Rye*)
6. abbreviations for titles given to people (Mr., Ms., Mrs., Hon., Rev., Dr., Ph.D., etc.).

Punctuation

apostrophe (')—shows either possession or the omission of a letter (*contractions*). When showing possession, the apostrophe often is followed by the letter "s."

EXAMPLE: Lincoln's "Emancipation Proclamation."

NOTE: The apostrophe is not added to possessive pronouns (hers, his, its, ours, theirs, yours).

CAUTION: "It's" is the contraction for "it is." In this case, the apostrophe shows that a letter has been omitted from a word. Because that word has been shortened or "contracted," it is called a contraction ("can't" for "cannot," "don't" for "do not, "won't" for "will not").

brackets ([ ])—show what was not in an original text, either spoken or written.

EXAMPLE: "The Eagle has landed [on the moon]."

CAUTION: Do not confuse brackets with parentheses.

colon (:)—introduces.

EXAMPLE: The Great Lakes have the following names: Superior, Michigan, Huron, Erie, and Ontario.

comma (,)—separates. Use a comma

1. after a succession of prepositional phrases when those phrases precede the main clause.

EXAMPLE: *On the fourth Thursday of November,*
Thanksgiving is celebrated.

2. after either a participial or an infinitive phrase when
   that phrase precedes the main clause.
   EXAMPLES:
   a. present participial phrase: *"Studying the DNA
      molecule,* Francis Crick and James Watson dis-
      covered its genetic code."
   b. past participial phrase: *"Inspired perhaps by the
      beauty of a winter evening,* the American poet
      Robert Frost wrote "Stopping by Woods on a
      Snowy Evening."
   c. infinitive phrase: *"To win a World Series title,* a
      baseball team must win four games out of a
      possible seven-game series."

3. after an adverb clause when that clause precedes the
   main clause.
   EXAMPLE: *"If this be treason,* make the most of it!"—
   Patrick Henry

4. before a coordinating conjunction when that conjunction connects two independent clauses.
   EXAMPLE: "Both read the same Bible and pray to the
   same God, *and* each invokes His aid against the
   other."—Abraham Lincoln

5. before and after nonessential information.
   EXAMPLE: George Washington, *the first President of
   the United States,* was born in Westmoreland
   County, Virginia.

6. between words, phrases, or clauses in a series.
   EXAMPLE: The couple packed up and moved *lock,
   stock, and barrel.*

7. between city and state/day and year.
   EXAMPLE: On *April 9, 1865,* Lee surrendered his
   army to Grant at *Appomattox Court House, Virginia.*

exclamation mark (!)—shows strong feeling.
EXAMPLE: "Off with their heads!"

parentheses (( ))—enclose information. That information usually is not as essential as the rest of the information in the phrase or clause.
EXAMPLE: Parentheses enclose information (but are not to be confused with brackets).

period (.)—ends a complete thought that is not an exclamation or a question.
EXAMPLE: "The pen is mightier than the sword."
NOTE: Periods also follow abbreviations.

question mark (?)—asks for information.
EXAMPLE: "What is art?"

quotation marks (" ")—enclose dialogue or titles of "small" works (poems, essays, short stories, etc.).
EXAMPLE of dialogue: President Kennedy said, "Ask not what your country can do for you but what you can do for your country."
EXAMPLE of title: "The Road Not Taken" is a famous poem by Robert Frost.
NOTE: Use single quotation marks (' ') to indicate a quotation within another quotation: " 'The Road Not Taken' is a poem by Robert Frost."
TIP: Titles of "large" works (novels, names of ships, etc.) are underlined or italicized.

semicolon (;)—connects information. Use a semicolon instead of a period between two independent clauses when those clauses are closely related to one another."
EXAMPLE: "Speech is silver; silence is golden."

Works Consulted

Abrams, M. H. *A Glossary of Literary Terms*. 5th ed. New York: Holt, Rinehart & Winston, 1988.

Achtert, Walter S., and Joseph Gibaldi. *MLA Style Manual*. New York: Modern Language Association, 1985.

Adventures for Readers, Book Two. Heritage ed. New York: Harcourt Brace Jovanovich, 1979.

Adventures in English Literature. Classic ed. New York: Harcourt Brace Jovanovich, 1979.

Atwell, Nancie. *In the Middle, Writing, Reading, and Learning with Adolescents*. Portsmouth, N.H.: Boynton/Cook, 1987.

Berthoff, Ann E. *Forming, Thinking, Writing*. Montclair, N.J.: Boynton/Cook, 1982.

Bloom, Allan. *The Closing of the American Mind*. New York: Simon and Schuster, 1987.

Brooks, Cleanth, and Robert Penn Warren. *Understanding Poetry*. 3rd ed. New York: Holt, Rinehart & Winston, 1967.

Booth, Wayne C. *The Rhetoric of Fiction*. Chicago: University of Chicago Press, 1973.

Burt, Forest D., and E. Clive Want, eds. *Invention and Design*. 4th ed. New York: Random House, 1985.

Cassill, R. V. *Writing Fiction*. 2nd ed. Englewood Cliffs, N.J.: Prentice-Hall, 1975.

Chicago Manual of Style. 13th ed. Chicago: University of Chicago Press, 1982.

Corbett, E. P. J. *The Little English Handbook*. 5th ed. New York: Wiley, 1987.

Dawe, Charles W., and Edward A. Dornan. *One to One, Resources for Conference-Centered Writing*. 3rd ed. Boston: Little, Brown, 1987.

Dornan, E. A., and Charles W. Dawe. *The Brief English Handbook*. Boston: Little, Brown, 1984.

Ehrlich, Eugene, and Daniel Murphy. *The Art of Technical Writing*. New York: Crowell, 1964.

Else, Gerald F. *Aristotle's Poetics: The Argument*. Cambridge, Mass.: Harvard University Press, 1963.

Fowler, H. W. *A Dictionary of Modern English Usage*. 2nd ed. Oxford: Oxford University Press, 1965.

French, C. W., Eileen Powell, and Howard Angione, eds. *The Associated Press Stylebook and Libel Manual*. 13th ed. New York: The Associated Press, 1982.

Frye, Northrop. *Anatomy of Criticism: Four Essays*. Princeton: Princeton University Press, 1957.

Griffith, Benjamin W. *A Pocket Guide to Literature and Language Terms*. Woodbury, N.Y.: Barron's, 1986.

Highet, Gilbert. *The Classical Tradition*. Oxford: Oxford University Press, 1970.

Hirsch, E. D., Jr. *Cultural Literacy*. Boston: Houghton Mifflin, 1987.

Hodges, John C., and Mary E. Whitten. *Harbrace College*

Handbook. 9th ed. New York: Harcourt Brace Jovanovich, 1984.

Holman, C. Hugh, William F. Thrall, and Addison Hibbard. *A Handbook to Literature.* Rev. ed. New York: Odyssey, 1960.

Jump, John D., ed. (1969–1976). *The Critical Idiom Series*, 48 vols. New York: Metheun, 1969–1987.

Kenner, Hugh. *The Art of Poetry.* New York: Rinehart, 1959.

Kirszner, Laurie G., and Stephen R. Mandell. *The Holt Handbook.* New York: Holt, Rinehart & Winston, 1986.

Kittredge, George L., and Frank E. Farley. *Advanced English Grammar.* Boston: Ginn, 1913.

Kuehner, Karen J., and John T. Reque. *Language Handbook.* Glenview, Ill.: Foreman, 1981.

Lazarus, Arnold, and H. Wendell Smith. *A Glossary of Literature and Composition.* Urbana, Ill.: NCTE, 1983.

Leggett, G., C. David Mead, and William Charvat. *Prentice-Hall Handbook for Writers.* 5th ed. Englewood Cliffs, N.J.: Prentice-Hall, 1970.

Martin, Harold C. *The Logic and Rhetoric of Exposition.* New York: Rinehart, 1959.

Montgomery County Public Schools Curriculum Guide (Grades 7–12). Rockville, Md.: MCPS, 1983.

Murray, James A., et al., eds. *The Oxford English Dictionary.* 13 vols. Oxford: Clarendon, 1888–1933.

Perrine, Laurence. *Sound and Sense.* 3rd ed. New York: Harcourt, Brace & World, 1969.

Petrosky, Anthony R., and David Bartholomae, eds. *The Teaching of Writing, Part II.* Chicago: NSSE, 1986.

Preminger, Alex, ed. *The Princeton Encyclopedia of Poetry and*

    Poetics. Rev. ed. Princeton: Princeton University Press, 1974.

Quiller-Couch, Arthur, ed. *The Oxford Book of Ballads*. Oxford: Oxford University Press, 1910.

The Random House Dictionary of the English Language, The Unabridged Edition. 2nd ed. New York: Random House, 1987.

Ravenel, William B. *English Reference Book*. 4th ed. Alexandria, Va.: Ravenel, 1959.

Reed, Herbert. *English Prose Style*. New York: Pantheon, 1980.

Scott, A. F. *Current Literary Terms*. 5th ed. New York: Macmillan, 1979.

Shapiro, Karl, and Robert Beum. *A Prosody Handbook*. New York: Harper & Row, 1965.

Shaw, Harry. *Concise Dictionary of Literary Terms*. 2nd ed. New York: McGraw-Hill, 1976.

———. *Errors in English*. 6th ed. New York: Barnes & Noble, 1967.

Strunk, William, Jr., and E.B. White. *The Elements of Style*. 3rd ed. New York: Macmillan, 1979.

Turabian, Kate L. *A Manual for Writers of Term Papers, Theses, and Dissertations*. 5th ed. Chicago: University of Chicago Press, 1987.

Warriner, John E., and Francis Griffith. *English Grammar and Composition, Complete Course*. Heritage ed. New York: Harcourt Brace Jovanovich, 1977.

Webster's New World Dictionary of the American Language. 2nd college ed. New York: Simon and Schuster, 1986.

Webster's Ninth New Collegiate Dictionary. Springfield, Mass.: Merriam-Webster, 1983.

Webster's II New Riverside University Dictionary. Boston: Houghton Mifflin, 1984.

Webster's Standard American Style Manual. Springfield, Mass.: Merriam-Webster, 1985.

West Des Moines Community School District Curriculum Guide (Grades 7–12). West Des Moines, Ia.: WDM Community School District, 1980.

Wimsatt, William K., and Cleanth Brooks. *Literary Criticism.* New York: Random House, 1957.

Woodson, L. *A Handbook of Modern Rhetorical Terms.* Urbana, Ill.: NCTE, 1979.

Index of the Terms

Note: Italicized terms are sub-entries included within main entries.

About The Authors

Stan Malless has taught literature, composition, and grammar (Grades 9–12) in the Montgomery County (Md.) Public Schools system; has also taught the talented and gifted (Grades 7–8) in the West Des Moines (Ia.) Community School District; and currently teaches composition and literature at Simpson College in Indianola, Ia. His poetry has appeared in *Antietam Review*, *The Antigonish Review*, *Orphic Lute*, and *Lyrical Iowa*. He lives in Des Moines with his wife, Phyllis, who teaches 8th-grade English at Stilwell JHS in West Des Moines.

Jeff McQuain has a Ph.D. in Literary Studies from The American University in Washington, D.C. He has taught college composition and literature at Montgomery Community College (Md.) and The American University. For the past five years he has been William Safire's research associate for the "On Language" column in *The New York Times*. He is also author of the syndicated daily newspaper feature "Our Language."